Coaching the Hogan Way

The Solution to Broken Leadership Development

by

Trish Kellett, MBA

Jackie Sahm, MS

Foreword by Dr. Robert Hogan

For information, contact Hogan Press
11 S. Greenwood, Tulsa OK 74120
hoganassessments.com

979-8-9856452-4-8

HOGANPRESS

Table of Contents

Foreword v

Introduction vii

Chapter 1: Leadership Development Shortfalls and Solutions 1

Element 1: Defining Leadership Incorrectly 1

Element 2: Measuring Circular Outcomes 4

Element 3: Chasing Moving Targets 7

Element 4: Taking a "One Size Fits All" Approach to Development 12

Element 5: Overlooking the Importance of Context 15

Element 6: Neglecting the Psychology of Behavior Change 19

Element 7: Decoupling Assessment and Development Activities 24

Chapter 2: The Hogan Coaching Protocol 27

Coach Selection 29

Chemistry Call 29

Phase 1: Context Gathering 29

Context Call 29

Get-Acquainted Call 30

Phase 2: Assessment and Feedback 32

Hogan Assessments and 360 Interviews 32

Integrated Feedback Session 33

Phase 3: Development Planning 34

Development Planning Meeting 34

Development Plan Finalization Meeting   36

Development Plan Alignment Meeting   38

Phase 4: Behavior Modification and Skill-Building   39

Ongoing Coaching Sessions   39

Phase 5: Evaluation and Ensuring Continued Success   40

Follow-up 360 Interviews   40

Wrap-up Meeting   40

Coaching Case Study: Moe   **43**

Appendices   **59**

Appendix 1: Coach's Notes from a Context Meeting   59

Appendix 2: Typical 360 Interview Questions   61

Appendix 3: Summary of Moe's 360 Interviews   63

Appendix 4: Moe's 360 Interview Questions   67

Appendix 5: Moe's Flash Report   68

About the Authors   **71**

Foreword

Leadership is the most important problem in human affairs. When good leaders are in place, organizations (countries, businesses, hospitals, schools, churches) flourish. When bad leadership is in place, everyone (except the elites) suffers. Leadership has been a hot topic in business for decades, and leadership literature is enormous—there are over 20,000 books on leadership in the Library of Congress. If you add to this, meaning all the leadership blogs, podcasts, and TED-talks in the cyber world, then it is staggering to consider the resources that have been devoted to leadership. Given this investment, one would think that leadership is well understood, but that is not the case. Issues with poor leadership have prevailed over the years. For example:

- 100% of the workforce say they have worked for an intolerable boss at some time.[1]

- 65% to 75% of U.S. workers say the worst, most stressful part of their job is their immediate boss.[2]

- 65% of the U.S. workforce say they would take a pay cut if someone would fire their boss.[3]

- About 80% of the global workforce (about 70% in the U.S.) say they are disengaged.[4]

Staff morale is the principal driver of business unit performance, which means that bad leadership causes massive financial losses each year. Putting the point differently, 90% of all new businesses fail and they fail due to bad leadership. The financial costs of bad leadership are immense.

Businesses invest billions of dollars in leadership development worldwide each year, but organizations continue to face leadership challenges. For example, 55% of CEOs say their biggest challenge is developing next-generation leaders.

We believe that leadership development is widely misunderstood, and that most leadership development programs are inadequate because of confusion about the definitions of leadership and personality and how they are related. Our approach to leadership development (Hogan Coaching) is a significant break from the past. Our model is based on five insights that challenge conventional thinking, but are supported by more than 30 years of research:

1. The definition of leadership. Leadership is **not** defined by a person's status in an organization; rather, it is defined by a person's ability to build, maintain, and motivate a high-performing team.

2. The definition of personality. Personality is **not** a set of traits; personality is two things. First it is your identity—the person you *think* you are. Second, it is your reputation—the person we *know* you are. Years of research on identity yielded no results. Research on reputation since 2000 has produced a cornucopia of useful findings about personality and success in life.

3. Personality matters tremendously. Research since 2000 shows that personality drives leadership—"who you are determines how you lead."

4. Strategic self-awareness (understanding how you are seen by others and how they react to those perceptions) is the key to behavioral changes that will make you a better leader.

5. Any productive intervention should begin with a proper assessment of a person's current capabilities—if you don't know where you are going, any road will get you there.

The rest of this book expands on these five insights. Enjoy.

Robert T. Hogan, PhD
Founder, Hogan Assessment Systems

Introduction

Adrian: Stellar Leader or a Problem in the Making?

Adrian was a highly successful vice president (VP) of sales at a Fortune 100 company. He impressed company executives from the day he was hired because of his presence, enthusiasm, charm, and ability to accomplish stretch sales goals that others thought were unrealistic. Early on, he was identified as high potential, and he moved through a number of sales assignments as he advanced to VP level, always making his success look easy. He was hand-picked for several executive education programs and leadership development initiatives, and he received glowing reports from the instructors of these. He was tapped for high-profile task forces where he received exposure to the C-suite and board who thought highly of him. When the company needed a polished speaker to address a community audience, Adrian was chosen. He truly was considered one of the best and the brightest in the talent pool for succession.

Adrian brought a consultant in to conduct a team development session with his direct reports. She flew in the day before and met with Adrian to interview him about the team and his goals for the session. He struck her as bright, passionate, and energetic—he spoke quickly with a kind of nervous intensity that was equal parts captivating and intimidating. The next morning, she arrived at headquarters an hour early to set up, and she was surprised to find Adrian's entire team of 10 direct reports already there having coffee in the boardroom. She began to see and hear obvious signs of team dysfunction within the first 5 minutes of walking through the door. She overheard one team member reveal that he had lost an incredibly valuable key customer account the night before. Another asked the group if anyone had spoken to Adrian yet this morning, and if so, what was the "temperature"? The question was answered by a woman whose eyes got wide and said, "it's definitely looking like a code red kind of day." They all agreed to wait until after the team session to share the bad news.

As the consultant readied the materials and listened to the exchange, the team was unknowingly revealing to her an elaborate system of tactics they had in place to manage Adrian's unpredictable temper and moods. His tendency to overreact to mistakes and setbacks created a downstream series of dysfunctional team habits designed to avoid the boss's anger. They walked on eggshells, withheld information, and concealed mistakes. When it came time to deliver bad news, they bargained amongst each other regarding whose turn it was to be the messenger and endure the "guillotine," as they called it. All of these tactics created an enormous amount of waste on the team that could have been spent more wisely elsewhere—wasted time, emotional energy, effort, and relationship capital. Adrian was smart, experienced, well-connected, and successful, yet he struggled to manage his intense personality, resulting in permanent damage to his team. Yet, this was completely unknown to his supporters at the highest levels of the organization.

As Adrian entered the boardroom, the shift in energy and tension in the room were immediately palpable—each team member displayed fear-based body language: crossed arms, avoiding eye contact, tense facial expressions, and the wringing of hands. The consultant recalled him saying in their conversation the day before, "It's better to be feared than loved, right?" with a smirk. Adrian was not a bad guy but he was definitely a bad boss. As an expert in personality and leadership, the consultant already had the Hogan assessment reports in a folder on the table that clearly explained the behaviors she was witnessing in the room. She took a deep breath and steeled herself for what was sure to be a very long day unpacking the dysfunction impacting this leader and his team.

She knew it was just a matter of time before Adrian's toxic leadership style caught up with him and his results began to suffer because of his team's disengagement. He had been able to hide this from his senior level fans until now, and they thought he was the future of the company, but a day of reckoning was sure to come.

On Leadership

Unfortunately, leaders such as Adrian aren't the exception; they are in our midst, impacting millions of lives and organizations every day. As Dr. Hogan related in the Foreword, incompetent leadership is the single most pressing problem facing humanity, and it is mind-boggling how many resources have been devoted to leadership over the years. Given this, one would think the leadership crisis would have been solved long ago, but it appears we have not moved the needle, as demonstrated by the alarming statistics Dr. Hogan shared.

Considering its widespread presence and its devastating impact on people, "bad leadership" is a public health crisis; yet leaders seem in a state of blissful ignorance regarding the sorry state of affairs. In fact, 80% of people think they are better than average leaders.[5]

Despite investing $366 billion worldwide in leadership development in 2019 ($166 billion in the U.S. alone), organizations continue to face a leadership challenge. Dr. Hogan cited that 55% of CEOs say their top challenge is developing next-generation leaders. This came ahead of concerns about economic recession (54%), product innovation (50%), and outperforming competitors (42%), among others.[6]

On Coaching

The business world has finally caught up to the sports, health, and fitness industries in realizing the following:

- Coaching works
- Coaching is a performance lever, not a last-ditch intervention.
- Coaching is equally necessary for Most Valuable Players and rookies.

- Coaching provides unmatched opportunities for feedback, insight, and accountability.

Just as elite athletes (Olympians, football players, tennis pros, etc.) rely on coaches to help them maximize their potential, so are leaders and senior executives harnessing the power of professional coaching to "up their game." However, there is still a lot of work to be done before these leaders become corporate "Olympic champions."

We at Hogan Assessment Systems (Hogan) believe leadership development is broken. Yes, broken—full stop, period. However, all is not lost, as we are confident that Hogan Coaching, our unique approach to leadership development, can fix it. In short:

LEADERSHIP DEVELOPMENT IS BROKEN!
HOGAN COACHING CAN FIX IT!

Hogan Coaching incorporates the five foundational concepts that Dr. Hogan outlined in the Foreword and bear repeating:

1. The definition of leadership. Leadership is **not** defined by a person's status in an organization; rather, it is defined by a person's ability to build, maintain, and motivate a high-performing team.

2. The definition of personality. Personality is **not** a set of traits; personality is two things. First it is your identity—the person you *think* you are. Second, it is your reputation—the person we *know* you are. Years of research on identity yielded no results. Research on reputation since 2000 has produced a cornucopia of useful findings about personality and success in life.

3. Personality matters tremendously. Research since 2000 shows that personality drives leadership—"who you are determines how you lead."

4. Strategic self-awareness (understanding how you are seen by others and how they react to those perceptions) is the key to behavioral changes that will make you a better leader.

5. Any productive intervention should begin with a proper assessment of a person's current capabilities—if you don't know where you are going, any road will get you there.

Using these five foundational elements, we have identified seven common shortfalls in leadership development that contribute to its "brokenness":

- Defining leadership incorrectly

- Measuring circular outcomes

- Chasing moving targets

- Taking a "one size fits all" approach to development

- Overlooking the importance of context

- Neglecting the psychology of behavior change

- Decoupling assessment and development activities

If these are the reasons leadership development is broken, then to fix it, we need to address these and replace them with elements that work. Hogan Coaching does exactly that. See Figure 1 for the shortfalls in leadership development and Hogan's solutions.

Figure 1

Shortfalls in Leadership Development and Hogan Solutions

Shortfall in Leadership Development	Hogan Solution
Defining leadership incorrectly	Redefine leadership
Measuring circular outcomes	Measure relevant outcomes
Chasing moving targets	Refocus on steady targets
Taking a "one size fits all" approach to development	Leverage individual differences via assessment data
Overlooking the importance of context	Treat context as paramount
Neglecting the psychology of behavior change	Change is hard; make it easier
Decoupling assessment and development activities	Fix the broken link between assessment and development activities

In the remainder of this book, we will explain each of these elements and its solution in greater detail. We will also demonstrate how these elements are addressed during Hogan Coaching. We will then do a deep dive into the Hogan Coaching protocol, including a case study to enable you to break the decades-long cycle of ineffective leadership development.

We think it is important for the reader to understand what this guide will NOT do in addition to what it will do. We will not teach people how to coach. We assume the reader is an experienced coach who is highly proficient in coaching techniques such as:

- Putting the leader at ease

- Creating a safe space for open discussion

- Honoring confidentiality

- Being non-judgmental

- Practicing superior listening skills

- Asking pertinent questions

- Inspiring reflection

- Using behavior- and evidence-based coaching

- Supporting the leader

- Challenging the leader when needed

- Encouraging learning and behavior modification

- Creating a development plan with metrics to measure progress

- Holding the leader accountable

- Possessing an expansive coaching "tool kit" that includes materials, models, exercises, readings, and the like that can be customized to the leader's needs

In addition, we will not teach people how to interpret and integrate the Hogan assessment reports. We assume the reader is a seasoned and proficient user of the Hogan instruments and reports:

Hogan Personality Inventory (HPI—the Potential Report): describes day-to-day leadership strengths; the "bright side" of personality.

Hogan Development Survey (HDS—the Challenge Report): addresses potential challenges or derailment risks that appear when under stress or complacent; the "dark side" of personality.

Motives, Values, Preferences Inventory (MVPI—the Values Report): highlights core values, drivers, and preferences, and predicts the kind of culture a leader will create; the "inside" of personality.

Flash Report—an overview of the HPI, HDS, and MVPI results.

We expect the reader to apply their well-honed coaching and stellar interpretation and integration skills within the Hogan Coaching protocol. We think the combination of these will turbocharge the coaching initiative and subsequent results. Furthermore, we expect the outcomes will astound you and the internal or external customers you serve.

Chapter 1

Leadership Development Shortfalls and Solutions

Element 1

Shortfall: Defining Leadership Incorrectly
Hogan Solution: Redefine Leadership

At Hogan, we believe the traditional definition of leadership is flawed. Historically, leadership has been defined by where a person sits in the organization's hierarchy. Regardless of whether a person was effective, they were considered a "leader" based on their position. Hogan defines leadership not by the position a person holds but as the ability to build, maintain, and motivate a team that outperforms the competition. Further, we view leadership as a resource for the group and not a source of privilege.

Leaders typically have been evaluated in individual terms such as decision-making, presence, communication skills, and the like, but we believe they should be evaluated in terms of the performance of their team. Good leaders build effective teams, and poor leaders destroy them. Leadership, then, is really about followership.

How Hogan Coaching Addresses This

Hogan Coaching takes this new definition into account by addressing the impact of the leader's strengths, development needs, and blind spots not only on their own performance, but also on their team's well-being and performance. Hogan Coaching shifts the lens so the leader gleans insights into their impact on their team and their team's ability to perform effectively. Hogan Coaching expands the leader's horizons beyond what they need to do for themselves to incorporate what they need to do for the team. We do this throughout the coaching initiative via context meetings, Hogan assessments, and 360 interviews, culminating in the creation of a development plan with development goals that significantly impact the team in addition to impacting the leader personally.

Often, a person is leading a team that is not composed of their direct reports, such as a cross-functional initiative or an ad hoc team. Regardless of reporting relationships, the person is still the leader who needs to view success through a team lens rather than an individual lens. Hogan Coaching is effective at addressing this as well as for a team of direct reports.

Case Story

Defining Leadership Incorrectly

Raphael, Vice President, Brand Management

Raphael, a Spanish national, was a seasoned multilingual executive with a worldwide Fortune 500 consumer goods company who had successfully completed assignments in several foreign countries. He was recognized as being highly creative, and the numerous marketing campaigns he had spearheaded were all highly successful. Further, he was viewed as a "hard-charger" who focused on achieving business results. His managers thought he was the epitome of a leader. Because of this and his past successes, he was seen as having the potential to be a corporate officer and was brought to the company's U.S. headquarters for further development. There, he was given a challenging assignment leading a large, highly talented team and overseeing all branding activities for a high-volume product line.

Soon after Raphael's arrival, it became readily apparent that his people management and relationship skills were lacking. He quickly developed a reputation for being brusque, unwilling to collaborate with peers, self-promoting, and unreceptive to others' ideas and points of view. Additionally, he was reluctant to delegate work and recognize the contributions of his highly capable direct reports. His results quickly began to falter, and his managers wondered if they had made a serious mistake.

The above situation was due to a flawed definition of leadership on the part of the executives who identified Raphael as officer material. They considered his individual attributes and accomplishments and his position in the hierarchy that involved managing people, but they didn't view leadership through a team lens to determine whether he could get things done through others. Had they asked his teams from prior positions for feedback, they would have uncovered his less than stellar interpersonal skills, and they could have addressed those prior to moving him into an "officer in waiting" role.

This phenomenon is so common it even has a nickname: the "Peter Principle." That is, organizations unwittingly promote people to the highest level of incompetence because they confuse a person's current performance with their potential effectiveness in broader roles with different demands. This self-perpetuating pattern can lead to organizations full of incompetent leaders. Research from the Corporate Executive Board supports this finding, estimating that 50% to 70% of executives fail within 18 months of being promoted.

Element 2

Shortfall: Measuring Circular Outcomes
Hogan Solution: Measure Relevant Outcomes

Too often, leadership development initiatives and executive coaching focus on outcomes we describe as "circular" or outcomes that are too narrow. Consistent with our view that leadership is all about followership, we believe outcomes should be focused on the team's performance and not merely on the leader's performance.

Typically, the success of leadership development programs is measured at their conclusion primarily by leader-centric measures such as:

- Did the leader like the program?

- Did the leader get promoted?

- Did the leader evaluate their progress positively in a subjective self-rating?

- Did the leader score well on performance ratings after the program?

Let's think about some of the preceding metrics for a moment because they lead to circular outcomes. How accurate are self-evaluations? Who decides whether to place a given leader in a high-potential leadership development program? Who does that leader's performance reviews? Who decides whether they get promoted? If your answers all point to the same one or two people, you recognize the gravity of the problem with most of these outcome measures. And the threats are not just in the measurement arena; we know that all people come programmed with a "similar-to-me" bias, one that results in a homogenous bench of talent which threatens higher-order diversity and inclusion goals in addition to matters of engagement and organizational effectiveness. The people making leadership succession decisions congratulate themselves on a job well-done, yet the outcomes were circular.

At Hogan, we believe these circular feel-good goals need to be replaced by specific measurable criteria that are relevant to development such as:

- Did the leader set actionable, relevant **change goals** that positively impacted the team?

- Did the leader **take action** on these goals following the program?

- Did any measure of **team effectiveness improve** following the program?

- Did the leader show any **improvement in post-program 360 scores**?

How Hogan Coaching Addresses This

Similar to the shift in measuring leadership development goals above, we employ a shift in how we measure the effectiveness of our coaching initiatives by viewing them through a team lens as well as an individual lens. At the conclusion of the coaching initiative, we want to know:

- Was the leader more self-aware of the impact of their behaviors on their team and other stakeholders?

- Did the leader achieve the behavior modifications described in their development plan based on evaluation by others?

- Did the post-coaching 360 survey of the leader's team and other stakeholders show progress from the initial 360?

- Did the team's engagement/satisfaction results improve?

- Did the team's business results improve?

- Was the leader's reputation enhanced based on evaluation by others?

In short, our evaluation of the success of the coaching initiative is team-focused and other-focused rather than merely leader-focused or contaminated by organizational politics.

Measuring Circular Outcomes

Tom, Director, Manufacturing

Tom was part of a leadership development program of a mid-sized manufacturer of heavy equipment. The participants in the program were identified as high-potential by executives, and the program was designed to groom them for senior-level positions. The focus was on rotating them through different departments to learn the business, thereby fast-tracking them to senior-level positions in a 5-year timeframe. Tom was extremely ambitious and wanted to get promoted rapidly, so he was grateful to be part of the leadership development program. He began his career in sales after receiving an MBA from a prestigious business school. He was highly successful in sales, and with the company executives, he gleaned a reputation of being "just the type of leader we need," as he was articulate, confident, and always well-dressed. Over the next 4 years he rotated through the marketing, finance, and public affairs departments, and he continued to do well. This reinforced the executives' opinion of him and of their ability to identify talent.

Tom's career was on track until he rotated into operations and was responsible for the manufacturing plants. The workers on the factory floor couldn't relate to him at all. He would walk through the plant and try to chat informally with them, but they thought he was "stiff," insincere, and lacking credibility. Behind his back, they laughed that he wouldn't know what to do with the equipment if he ever had to use it because it seemed that he didn't like to get his hands dirty. Further, they jested that even his jeans were pressed, and they bet he went for a salon blowout every morning, as he never had a hair out of place. In short, he was "too perfect" and just couldn't bond with his most important audience—his extended team.

This classic "suits vs. boots" situation could have been avoided had both the company executives and the leadership development program not been so focused on getting Tom promoted. Had they instead focused on how he could relate to and build credibility with his team and organization, Tom could have honed his trust-building skills prior to rotating into the operations role. The executives measured Tom by their insular "circular" standards that he was "a star" rather than by objective measures or input from others.

Element 3

Shortfall: Chasing Moving Targets
Hogan Solution: Refocus on Steady Targets

Many times, leadership development initiatives, including coaching, are focused on constantly moving targets that are anchored by the current leadership fads, books, buzzwords, or human resources (HR) crazes. As examples, remember grit, matrix management, learning agility, growth mindset, strategic thinking, and managing change? These fads distract leaders from what they should be focused on: developing solid, foundational leadership skills that will positively impact their teams.

In addition to fads, leadership development initiatives, including coaching, have also historically been based on leadership competency models.

The problem with competency models, no matter how well-researched, is that they lead to the black-and-white thinking that a leader either has or does not have a competency. This leads to conclusions that presence of a competency is "good" and absence is "bad," that "more is better," and other fallacious judgments as depicted below in Figure 2:

Figure 2

Leadership Development Competencies

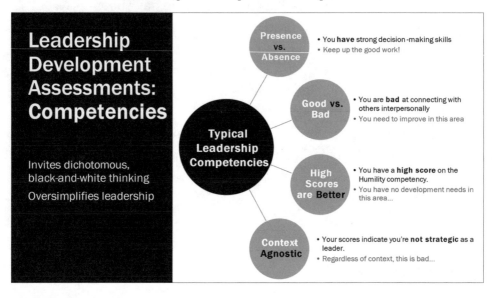

At Hogan, we believe the competency model approach oversimplifies leadership. To address the problems shown in the figure, we created the Hogan Leadership Model, a well-researched and statistically valid model correlated with scales from the three Hogan assessment instruments (Hogan Personality Inventory [HPI], Hogan Development Survey [HDS], and Motives, Values, Preferences Inventory [MVPI]). Our model is based on four universal domains that demand a leader's time and attention. There are two dimensions under each domain (eight total dimensions) and two behaviors under each dimension (16 total behaviors). The Hogan Leadership Model does not judge *if* a leader has a competency, but rather *how* a behavior unfolds. The model is context-based and allows for nuanced interpretation. See Figure 3.

Figure 3

The Hogan Leadership Model

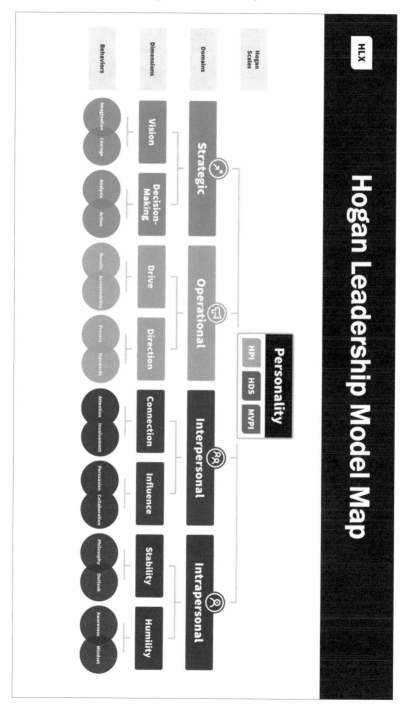

How Hogan Coaching Addresses This

Hogan Coaching focuses on the four domains and the associated dimensions and behaviors depicted in Figure 3. These four domains are foundational to leadership, and they are the areas that typically demand a leader's attention regardless of the "flavor of the month" leadership fad. Furthermore, we focus on *how* the leader approaches the domains and exhibits the behaviors, not on *if* they do so, thereby avoiding the traditional bipolar thinking of *have* or *have not*. Because context is all-important, we tailor our coaching targets (behavior modifications and skill acquisition) to the leader's unique situation and to the needs of the team.

When a client has a leadership model or a competency model they want the Hogan coach to use as a framework, we can do so. However, we still take the approach of *how* the behavior is demonstrated, not *if* it is demonstrated.

Case Story

Chasing Moving Targets

Juanita, Senior Director, Procurement

Juanita was a senior director of procurement for a multinational pharmaceutical company. She had an excellent reputation and was always rated "exceeds expectations" on her yearly appraisal. Her team liked and respected her, she had very little employee turnover, and her employee engagement scores were in the top 5% of the company every year. Juanita was somewhat shy and soft-spoken, hard-working, and modest, which was a good fit for her relatively low-profile role.

The company adopted a new leadership model, and one of the competencies stressed the most was "leading from the front." Part of its definition was being visible, speaking up, being innovative, and subsequently being recognized for new ideas—in short, having a high profile. Juanita's manager and other higher-ups thought she had potential, but they saw her low-key manner as a dealbreaker given the new competency model. They advised her that she needed to significantly increase her visibility and profile if she wanted to continue to progress. What they failed to realize was that there are different ways to "lead from the front," and Juanita's team believed she was indeed leading from the front—she just approached it in a different manner and less aggressively than the competency model described. Juanita became disengaged because of this, and her team subsequently did as well. What had been a well-oiled machine began to show signs of rust.

This could have been avoided if Juanita's management had realized that leadership comes in different packages and that "leading from the front" could be demonstrated in different ways rather than only by a cookie-cutter approach. While Juanita's way of leading from the front didn't match management's definition, she was very effective in building a high-performing team. It was counterproductive for her to chase the moving target of "leading from the front."

Element 4

Shortfall: Taking a "One Size Fits All" Approach to Development
Hogan Solution: Leverage Individual Differences via Assessment Data

One of the core beliefs of Hogan is "who you are determines how you lead." Therefore, a leader's personality that reveals *who* they are is crucial in determining *how* they will lead. Leaders and their personalities are unique, and one size *does not* fit all. Cookie-cutter approaches to coaching and development are doomed to failure. Individual differences in strengths, watch-outs, and blind spots need to be identified and addressed in any development process. This is best done through our valid, reliable assessment instruments: the HPI, HDS, and MVPI. They reveal people's strengths and sweet spots, the behaviors that can make them less effective as leaders, and their values, especially the kind of culture they will create as a leader.

Assessment data are an absolutely critical diagnostic tool for a coach to use. Not having assessment data as a foundation is similar to a doctor prescribing medicine without establishing the root causes of the patient's issue. Further, if the coach relies solely on the leader for input regarding the situation and issues, it is akin to a patient diagnosing themselves and telling the doctor what to prescribe.

How Hogan Coaching Addresses This

All Hogan Coaching initiatives begin with the administration of the HPI, HDS, and MVPI instruments. These reveal the uniqueness of the leader's personality. Even if two leaders have the same score on a scale, they will not necessarily behave the same way due to having different subscale scores or the way the scale interacts with other scales. To complement the Hogan instruments, other assessments such as written 360 surveys, 360 interviews with key stakeholders, business simulations, assessment centers, and the like can be added. They will all help highlight the leader's uniqueness and the most impactful areas to address. They provide a baseline to which the leader can be compared later to determine the success of the initiative.

Case Story

Taking a "One Size Fits All Approach" to Development

Priyanka, Vice President, Product Development

Priyanka was a vice president of product development at a multibillion-dollar consumer products company known for its innovation and repeated success in introducing new products. Priyanka thrived there because she was highly creative and innovative, big-picture oriented, and adept at setting business strategy. She seemed to be able to "see around corners" to anticipate what customers wanted in new features and products. Her team admired her creativity, constant flow of new ideas, and ability to see the big picture. Further, they truly liked and respected her. However, they felt at times she could overuse these strengths, which sometimes became "too much of a good thing." She was so creative and innovative that she could appear scattered and unfocused. When direct reports would bring a proposal to her, she would immediately go into strategy and innovation mode, saying things like "Have you thought of this? Have you thought of that? Did you consult so-and-so? Did you read such-and-such article?" This was very off-putting to her direct reports because they felt their ideas were being questioned, worried they appeared unprepared, and ultimately felt they had disappointed her. In reality, she was just thinking out loud and trying to be helpful.

To make sure they maintained their competitive edge, the company sponsored a leadership development program for high potentials focused on strategic thinking and innovation, one of their three key leadership imperatives. They arranged for professors from a top-notch business school to teach courses on strategic thinking and innovation for a half-day each month over a period of 6 months. Further, participants were divided into small groups and given a real-world strategy and innovation issue facing the company for which they needed to find a solution and present it to the board.

Even though Priyanka didn't need to build strategic thinking and innovation skills, she was selected for the program because she was deemed high potential. Although she truly shined in the course, this program caused Priyanka to overuse her strengths even more and did not serve her development needs. She and her team would have been much better served had she embarked on a development initiative that addressed her interpersonal and communication skills. Unfortunately, the company assumed all participants had the same development needs due to taking to a common, but misled, "one-size-fits-all" approach to both the creation of leadership competency models and the development programs designed to prop them up.

Element 5

Shortfall: Overlooking the Importance of Context
Hogan Solution: Treat Context as Paramount

At Hogan, we believe "one size fits none," and leadership development initiatives are doomed to fail if the leader's context is overlooked. To determine what the leader needs to do (or not do) to be more effective and to make the team more successful, context is key. The context within which the leader is operating must be understood to tailor the development initiative. The four major elements to consider are the following:

1. **The leader's role**: Which leadership domains, dimensions, and behaviors from the Hogan Leadership Model are the most important to succeed in the role?
   For example, the skills and behaviors required for a leader in a marketing role are very different than the ones required for a leader in a tax attorney's role.

2. **The leader's team**: What is the experience level of the team? The dynamics? The morale? The motivation level?
   For example, a team of inexperienced "newbies" will have much different needs from their leader than a team of experienced professionals.

3. **The leader's manager**: What is the personality of the leader's manager? Their values? Their likes and dislikes?
   For example, if a leader is high Colorful and their manager is high Colorful as well, the manager might view the leader as very entertaining, whereas a manager who is low Colorful might view the leader as a "showboat."

4. **The organization's culture**: What "is it like around here"? Which behaviors are rewarded? What are the taboos?

   For example, behaviors that are derailers in one culture might not be derailers in another. High Imaginative might be a derailer in a staid engineering culture but not at all in an advertising agency.

How Hogan Coaching Addresses This

Hogan Coaching incorporates context throughout the initiative. The initiative begins with a context meeting between the coach, the leader's manager, and HR sponsor to obtain their perspectives of the reasons the leader is being sponsored for coaching and their views of the leader's context. This meeting is followed by a context meeting between the Hogan coach and the leader so the coach can glean the leader's perspective. Only after the coach conducts these meetings to understand the leader's context fully can the coach tailor the coaching initiative. Context is used throughout the remainder of the coaching initiative in interpreting the assessment data, determining 360 interview questions, creating the most impactful development goals, and creating the content of the coaching sessions.

Often, context isn't static, and the coach will need to help the leader navigate any changes in context that occur as the coaching initiative progresses. For example, mid-way through the initiative, there might be a reorganization that results in the leader having a new manager. Based on the new manager's personality and preferences, the leader will need to consider behavior modifications they should make to ensure the most productive working relationship.

Overlooking the Importance of Context

David, Vice President, Marketing

David was a high-potential marketing vice president for a division of a consumer products company and was being groomed for the division's Chief Marketing Officer role. He was known for being extremely creative and innovative, creating some of the most successful marketing campaigns the company had ever implemented. His direct reports were inspired by him to achieve their goals thanks to his contagious enthusiasm and the inclusive culture he created. In addition, he was collaborative with his peers, and they viewed him as a true partner and subject matter expert for their marketing needs. He was highly successful in the relaxed and collaborative culture that was the hallmark of the division in which he worked.

However, when David started making presentations to the executive team and board of directors of the entire company, they began to question his ability to hold the future position of CMO. Their feedback focused on his overly casual approach, as he would address them as "you guys," and his style was described as very "folksy" in a recent 360. Further, he confused them with his excessive use of technical marketing terms that they didn't understand. They described his responses to their questions as scattered and unprepared, and they felt he didn't clearly articulate a vision or represent the "voice of marketing." In short, they didn't think he had the gravitas needed to be successful in the C-suite.

David failed to recognize that his context changed significantly the minute he walked into the boardroom to deliver a presentation to that group. The board members were much more serious, scrutinizing, and business-focused than what he was comfortable with in his division's more casual culture. His development should have focused on self-awareness and situational awareness and how to flex his style.

Sylvia, Senior Director, Strategy

Sylvia was a senior director of strategy for a division of a global pharmaceutical company. She had worked closely with the CEO of the division when she was a consultant with a premier management consulting firm hired to optimize the business. The CEO valued Sylvia's advice so much that he hired her into the division as his chief of staff. Sylvia excelled at providing solid advice to the CEO, she prepared compelling PowerPoint presentations and speeches for the CEO to use, and she was highly regarded by the rest of the C-suite as well. They particularly valued her ability to be objective about decisions and "cut to the chase" without letting emotion enter into discussions.

After 18 months, the CEO moved Sylvia into the role of senior director of strategy because she was such a big thinker and also to give her greater exposure to the organization. Sylvia's ability to be objective and unemotional, which had gained her admiration in the chief of staff job, now was leading to her downfall. Her peers thought she was too "clinical" and acted too much like a consultant rather than an employee. Further, they believed she didn't have the best interests of the business or employees at heart. At one point, the division needed to downsize, and they felt Sylvia was entirely too cold and calculating about eliminating jobs and didn't consider the human aspect at all.

Sylvia's development should have included helping her realize how her context had changed and that she needed to identify new behaviors to be successful in her new environment.

Element 6

Shortfall: Neglecting the Psychology of Behavior Change
Hogan Solution: Change Is Hard; Make It Easier

A universal truth is that change is hard. If it were easy, an entire publishing niche of "how-to" books and motivational guides would disappear! How simple it would be if people just made up their minds to change behaviors (e.g., New Year's resolutions), and that was all it took. Poof—like magic, the behavior would change with no effort. Of course, that is not the case, and people continue to struggle with breaking bad habits and starting new ones. It's been said that behavior change requires two people—one to do it and one to notice. Lack of ongoing feedback is often a problem in behavior change as positive reinforcement is key to motivating change.

Many leadership development and coaching programs overlook the fact that long-term behavioral change requires leaders to have both the motivation and the ability to change. Unrealistic goals, limited resources (including time and energy), and a lack of feedback can inhibit a leader's successful development. This can be demotivating, which is especially problematic if a leader is ambivalent to development or struggles with self-awareness in the first place.

Complicating matters are that many competency models are aspirational and therefore unclear or paradoxical. Leaders are told they need to be "strategic and innovative" yet "process-oriented and operational," or they're told to "think outside the box" but to "be practical," as well. Such conflicting directions make behavior change even more elusive.

How Hogan Coaching Addresses This

At Hogan, we believe behavior change is made easier via the following steps, and we incorporate these into our coaching protocol:

1. Increase the leader's strategic self-awareness regarding their reputation versus their identity. This is done through use of the valid Hogan assessments.

2. Connect the needed changes to achieving the reputation they want to have.

3. Confront any ambivalence the leader has around behavior change. If the leader feels they must give up a behavior that has made them successful thus far, they will likely be reluctant to do it. Assure them that they rarely need to abandon a behavior completely, but rather, they need to make more subtle adjustments.

4. Find ways to make development easier using the following approaches:

   - Increase **motivation** to do the behavior

   - Decrease **difficulty** of the behavior

   - Increase **ability** to do the behavior

   - Increase **reward** for doing the behavior

   - Build in cues to **prompt** the behavior

5. Connect the needed changes to accomplishing a business goal that is important to the leader and their team.

6. Find a "hook" that will motivate the leader to change. The leader's Hogan results can provide valuable insights into this (e.g., a person high on Altruism might resonate with the fact that the behavior change will help people be more successful, or a high Ambition leader might relate to the behavior change accelerating the achievement of results).

7. Clearly define what the needed changes are and what they look like in the leader's everyday world.

8. Select behavior modifications that will not be resource-constrained, as time and effort are always at a premium. Identify development activities the leader can practice as part of their everyday job and not as an add-on to their already busy schedule. If a leader needs to enhance their communication skills, a much more viable development activity is to practice in their staff meetings rather than taking a public speaking course.

9. Start with small pivots and baby steps, not giant steps. Many times, development goals are flawed, such as the following common mistakes:

Common Mistakes: Change Goals	Examples
Overly ambitious change goals	*I want to quit smoking and drinking this week.*
Too vague or broad	*I want to be more strategic as a leader.*
Unrealistic	*I want to be a CEO by age 30.*
Not measurable	*I want to lose weight.*
Lacking ability	*I want to do a couch-to-Ironman program.*
Overcorrection	*I want to be more assertive!* *(Dramatically overdoes it.)*

10. Look for early wins that will reinforce the value of the behavior change.

11. Encourage the leader to enlist a trusted colleague to provide honest feedback on a continuing basis.

12. Consider conducting a "pulse check" with selected stakeholders at the midway point of the coaching initiative to gauge progress.

Further, the Hogan coach is available to the leader during the entire coaching journey to point out self-deception or ambivalence should they occur, to offer guidance on reputation enhancement and management, and to address any resource constraints.

Case Story

Neglecting the Psychology of Behavior Change

James, Director, Accounting

James was a director of accounting for a high-tech software firm. He was an introvert by nature, soft-spoken and serious. While he communicated frequently with his small team, it was mostly via email or text, and he never wasted words. He was a recognized subject matter expert in a niche area of accounting, and he was always helping his direct reports learn and grow in the area and take on new responsibilities. They valued his direction and support and appreciated his calm, direct style. James was known for setting high goals and then delivering on them because of his laser focus. He and his team never missed a due date, and their work was reliable and accurate. James's manager (the vice president of accounting) and skip-level manager (the CFO) thought

James was underutilized and was capable of taking on more responsibility. They were concerned, however, about his quiet, low-key approach and apparent lack of confidence when he spoke. They hired a coach to work with James to polish his communication skills and executive presence in general.

James was flattered that the senior executives thought he was capable of bigger and better things, and he willingly accepted the coaching opportunity. He was ambitious, and he addressed his development goals with the same determination he applied to his business goals. Unfortunately, instead of starting small with some readily doable behavior modifications, he selected too many goals that were too much of a reach. He enrolled in a public speaking class, joined a civic organization that focused on public speaking, volunteered for speaking engagements in the community, and became an adjunct professor at a local college. He was spread so thin and so far out of his comfort zone that he became completely discouraged and burned out. The development journey he had begun happily soon became an energy-draining trudge.

Rather than setting his sights so high initially, James should have started with small, attainable behavior changes he could implement in a familiar space. For example, he could have chosen development actions such as having a one-on-one conversation with each direct report each week and being a guest presenter at each peer's staff meeting once a month. Once he was comfortable with these and gained confidence, he could have built on these successes to move on to more difficult development opportunities in foreign environments.

Element 7

Shortfall: Decoupling Assessment and Development Activities
Hogan Solution: Fix the Broken Link between Assessment and Development Activities

Too often, leadership development involves an assessment or two, creation of a development plan, some learning experiences or skill building, and perhaps a coaching component. If these do not connect, the overall program probably makes about as much sense as a box of puzzle pieces. Many times, the development program comprises discrete events such as an individualized assessment followed by separate learning experiences that are not necessarily connected. Or, sometimes, every leader moves through identical program steps, all focused on the same competencies without linkage between the program components.

Instead, think about the experience of working with a personal trainer. The first step, assessment, gives the trainer the information they need to offer the client personalized education and design a unique fitness plan for them to apply. If the trainer is effective, each new component will build on the previous one. Then the trainer will check in on the client's progress regularly, adjusting as needed.

How Hogan Coaching Addresses This

The Hogan coach is the equivalent of the personal trainer in the example above. The coach customizes the initiative to the leader throughout the journey and makes adjustments as needed. Leaders first acquire self-knowledge through assessment feedback, gaining an understanding of how others are likely to perceive their strengths and opportunities for improvement. With their coach, they determine which behavior changes will be most impactful for them personally, their team, and the broader organization given the relevant context. They then incorporate both the assessment insights and prioritized behavior changes into their learning experiences and development plans. They not only identify what they need to do through assessment, but they acquire knowledge through learning, and then apply it as part of their development. The entire process is seamless—the puzzle pieces now fit together rather being discrete events. Assessment, learning, development, and behavior change become a "thread" in their leadership journey.

Case Story

Decoupling Assessment and Development Activities

Max, Plant Manager

Max was the manager of a plant making high-precision medical devices that had to conform to very narrow tolerances. Max's plant consistently led the company's other plants in quality. This was partly due to Max's team of experienced operators and partly due to his rigorous enforcement of proven manufacturing processes.

The company was undergoing some major changes, and they created a leadership development program designed to assist leaders in dealing with change and ambiguity. The program consisted of the Hogan assessments, classroom sessions addressing change and ambiguity, and the creation of a development plan to be presented to the executive sponsors.

Max's assessment results revealed he wasn't naturally wired to deal easily with change and ambiguity. His 360 confirmed this behavioral tendency, with all respondents acknowledging how Max's greatest strength of being precise and exact could also be his Achilles' heel at times. Even so, he actively participated in the classroom activities and viewed the leadership development program as an opportunity to grow. His development plan included reading books and attending webinars on change and ambiguity in addition to some personal goals to avoid overusing his strengths. However, he was not coached or encouraged to include any job-related or business-related goals to which he could actually apply what he had learned.

Max's experience was typical of a disconnected development process, because as a plant manager required to enforce tried-and-true protocols, he had no organic opportunities to apply the change and ambiguity management skills he had acquired. This disconnect could have been avoided had Max been paired with a Hogan coach who had expertise in assessment-based coaching designed to create behavioral actions that connect assessment to development. Unfortunately, Max was assigned to an internal coach with very little experience using the Hogan assessments and linking them to 360 results. Although the hard cost of retaining a highly skilled external coach is generally higher than deploying internal coaching resources, the opportunity cost of leaving that much value on the table likely neutralizes any savings.

Chapter 2

The Hogan Coaching Protocol

In the preceding chapter, we addressed the seven shortfalls of leadership development and how Hogan Coaching incorporates each of the fixes into our protocol. In this chapter, we will take a different view and describe the Hogan Coaching protocol in the order in which each step occurs and relate it to the fixes. Every step in the protocol incorporates **almost all** the fixes to ensure the coaching initiative is successful. The protocol described below and shown in Figure 4 is for a typical 6-month executive coaching initiative. The timeline varies depending on the availability of the 360 respondents, but typically Phases 1, 2, and 3 take 6 weeks to 2 months which leaves 4 to 4½ months for Phases 4 and 5. The fixes each step addresses are shown in Figure 5.

Figure 4

The Hogan Coaching Protocol

Coach Selection

- Chemistry Call between Coach and Leader

Phase 1: Context Gathering

- Context Call between Coach, Leader's Manager, and HR Sponsor
- Get-Acquainted Call between Coach and Leader

Phase 2: Assessment and Feedback

- Hogan Assessments and 360 Interviews
- Integrated Feedback Session

Phase 3: Development Planning

- Development Planning Meeting
- Development Plan Finalization Meeting
- Development Plan Alignment Meeting

Phase 4: Behavior Modification and Skill-Building

- Ongoing Coaching Sessions

Phase 5: Evaluation and Ensuring Continued Success

- Follow-up 360 Interviews
- Wrap-Up Meeting between Leader, Coach, Leader's Manager, and HR Sponsor

Figure 5

Mapping of Leadership Development Solutions to Hogan Coaching Protocol

Hogan Leadership Development Solution	Chemistry Call	Context Call	Get-Acquainted Call	Hogan LFS Assessments	360 Interviews	Integrated Feedback Session	Development Planning Meeting	Development Plan Creation	Development Plan Alignment	Ongoing Coaching Sessions	Follow-up 360 Interviews	Wrap-up Meeting
Redefine Leadership		●	●	●	●	●	●	●	●	●	●	●
Measure Relevant Outcomes		●	●	●	●	●	●	●	●	●	●	●
Refocus on Steady Targets		●	●	●	●	●	●	●	●	●	●	●
Leverage Individual Differences	●			●	●	●	●	●	●	●	●	●
Treat Context as Paramount	●	●	●	●	●	●	●	●	●	●	●	●
Make Change Easier					●	●	●	●	●	●	●	●
Fix the Broken Link						●	●	●	●	●	●	●

Coach Selection

Chemistry Call

The relationship between the coach and the leader is crucial to the success of a coaching initiative. It is key that the leader trust the coach, feel comfortable opening up to the coach, respect what the coach recommends, and feel a sense of compatibility with the coach overall. In short, there needs to be a "bond" or "chemistry" between the two for coaching to be maximally successful. It's also important for the leader to feel that they have a voice in choosing their coach rather than being assigned one by their manager or HR person. At Hogan, we provide four to six coach bios to the leader, and the leader narrows the field to two to three with whom they would like to have a brief "chemistry call" to check for fit. Typically, the calls are 30 minutes or less, but they enable the leader to determine which coach best meets their individual personality, context, and overall needs. Once the leader has chosen a coach, then the coaching initiative can begin.

Fixes Addressed: Leverage Individual Differences; Treat Context as Paramount

Phase 1: Context Gathering

Context Call

At Hogan, we involve key stakeholders such as the leader's manager and HR sponsor throughout the coaching process. This ensures that all parties (manager, HR sponsor, coach, and leader) are aligned regarding what needs to be accomplished during the coaching to ensure there are no surprises at the end of the engagement. To obtain background and context, the coach must first meet with the leader's manager and

HR sponsor. Usually an hour in length, this call is an opportunity for the manager and HR sponsor to provide their perspectives on topics such as:

1. Background on the organization, including culture, business goals and objectives, and challenges

2. The reason for identifying the leader for coaching

3. The leader's key strengths, areas for development, and blind spots

4. The leader's reputation

5. Behaviors most important for the leader to modify or leverage to positively impact the team

6. The leader's attitude toward coaching and feedback, and their coachability

7. The leader's performance and potential within the organization

8. How they define "success" for the coaching initiative

Further, the meeting provides an opportunity for the coach to explain the coaching protocol (timelines, number of sessions, etc.), that confidentiality will be honored at all times (the coach will report on process, not content of the sessions), and roles and responsibilities (e.g., in addition to providing ongoing support to the leader, the manager and HR sponsor will need to approve the list of 360 interview respondents).

An example of a coach's notes from a Context Meeting is available in Appendix 1.

Fixes Addressed: Redefine Leadership; Measure Relevant Outcomes; Refocus on Steady Targets; Treat Context as Paramount

Get-Acquainted Call

Soon after the context call with the manager and HR sponsor, the coach and leader connect to get better acquainted and to launch their work together. They will have first met on the chemistry call, and this get-acquainted call will provide the opportunity to bond further. While the context call with the manager and HR sponsor provided the coach with their perspectives, this call provides the coach with the leader's perspective on many of the same topics. If there is a disconnect among the parties, the coach needs to know about it early on. The call also serves to deepen the leader-coach relationship, as the topics covered lend themselves to sharing and reflection. Typical topics include the leader's:

1. Background (a brief life history), including personal and career aspects

2. Career aspirations

3. Context within which they are operating

4. View of their key strengths, areas for development, motivators, and values

5. View of their reputation

6. Major business objectives and challenges

7. Assessment of their team's ability and performance level and how they can most positively impact it

8. Understanding of why they were selected for, or requested coaching

9. Definition of success of the coaching initiative

10. Concerns or questions about the coaching initiative

In addition to the above, the coach will assure the leader of confidentiality throughout the engagement. Further, the coach will clarify roles and responsibilities, identify support needed, and explain the coaching protocol, including asking the leader to identify eight to ten people for the 360 interviews.

Fixes Addressed: Redefine Leadership; Measure Relevant Outcomes; Refocus on Steady Targets; Treat Context as Paramount

Phase 2: Assessment and Feedback

Hogan Assessments and 360 Interviews

After the get-acquainted meeting, the leader takes the HPI, HDS, and MVPI assessments, and the respective Potential, Challenge, Values, and Flash reports are generated. These assessments are complemented by 360 interviews conducted by the coach with key stakeholders. At the get-acquainted meeting, the coach asks the leader to select a 360 audience of eight to ten people. These should be people who have sufficient interaction with the leader to be able to give the coach behavioral examples of strengths, areas for development, and blind spots. They should be objective (e.g., not a "best friend" or someone "with an axe to grind"), and they should be people whose input the leader will respect and heed. The leader's manager and HR sponsor approve the list.

After the leader advises the 360 audience that they will be hearing from the coach, the coach contacts each respondent and asks them questions about the leader's strengths, areas for development, and leadership style in general. Not all questions are appropriate for every coaching endeavor, and in addition, time does not permit asking all questions, as the interviews are typically 1 hour. So the participant and coach select a subset of the questions that will provide the most meaningful insights. Further, the questions can be customized if there is something the leader is curious about. See Appendix 2 for typical questions, including examples of modifications. Once the 360 interviews are completed, the coach summarizes the results, preserving the anonymity of the respondents. See Appendix 3 for an example of a completed 360 interview summary.

Fixes Addressed: Redefine Leadership; Measure Relevant Outcomes; Refocus on Steady Targets; Leverage Individual Differences; Treat Context as Paramount; Make Change Easier

Integrated Feedback Session

The word to be emphasized in this step is "integrated" because it is through the integration of the results from the Hogan assessments and the comments from the 360 interviews that a clear picture of strengths, areas for development, and blind spots is obtained. The 360 interviews reveal how the Hogan results manifest in the real world. The combination provides powerful insights into behaviors that need to be leveraged or modified and how easy or difficult it will be for the leader to change them. The 360 input also provides perspective as to which behaviors are a priority to change due to their greater impact.

If appropriate, the feedback session for the Hogan assessments can be conducted ahead of the 360 feedback session. This provides the leader several days or weeks to process what they heard in the Hogan feedback session. The 360 feedback session then covers the 360 information and integrates it with the Hogan feedback, which is a very powerful way to identify themes and priorities for change. After receiving the integrated feedback, the leader needs an opportunity to process it and reflect on which major takeaways will have the most significant impact on their team. Once this is done, the creation of a development plan can begin.

Note: The coach should also receive copies of written 360 survey results, performance reviews, development plans, employee engagement survey results, and any other documents or reviews that have been done within the past year if they will inform the coaching. Those can be used to inform the integrated feedback discussion as well.

Fixes Addressed: Redefine Leadership; Measure Relevant Outcomes; Refocus on Steady Targets; Leverage Individual Differences; Treat Context as Paramount; Make Change Easier

Phase 3: Development Planning

Development Planning Meeting

While major takeaways are identified during the integrated feedback session, it is typically premature to decide on two to three development goals for the development plan at this time. The leader needs to reflect upon the feedback and discuss it with the coach to determine which behavior changes will be most impactful for their team and the broader business. We recommend selecting two to three development goals that are either strengths to leverage, watch-outs to rein in, or blind spots to address. Setting more than three goals can cause the leader's efforts, including time and energy, to be spread too thin to make noticeable progress.

The leader and coach assess the difficulty of the behavior changes identified, the resources needed, the urgency of the changes, and other contextual issues to decide on the development goals. This session is usually a rich exchange of ideas between the leader and the coach regarding development targets, possible action items associated with each, and what "success" would look like. At the end of the session, the leader has enough information to create the first draft of their development plan.

As for the development plan—the form itself—there are many different formats, but the effective ones include the following elements:

- Development goals, including what success looks like (the desired state)

- Specific behaviors to modify, be they strengths to leverage or watch-outs to rein in, which should be directly linked to team performance and business results

- Specific actions to take to drive the behavior modification

- Support and resources needed from the leader's manager and others

- Measures, both quantitative and qualitative, to determine progress and ultimate success

- Timeline

Hogan recommends that the leader use the organization's standard form if they have one, so the development plan associated with coaching is not an "application" on top of their regular development plan. If the organization does not have a preferred form, Hogan recommends the one shown in Figure 6.

Figure 6

Blank Development Plan Form

NAME:

MANAGER:

Development Goal	Actions	Measures Of Success	Time Frame

Fixes Addressed: Redefine Leadership; Measure Relevant Outcomes; Refocus on Steady Targets; Leverage Individual Differences; Treat Context as Paramount; Make Change Easier; Fix the Broken Link

Development Plan Finalization Meeting

Typically, after the development planning meeting, the leader emails the first draft of their plan to the coach, who makes comments and suggestions and emails it back; several iterations of this can occur. By the finalization meeting, the development plan should be almost done, so the goal is to "polish" the plan into a version to share with the leader's manager and HR sponsor. The development plan is an ideal vehicle to "Fix the Broken Link," as the goals and actions and measures of success identified are connected to the team, the business, and the learning experience in a seamless fashion.

It is key that the leader feel ownership for the development plan, so they need to be the author of it, with the coach providing advice and counsel. Under no circumstances should the coach actually create the development plan for the leader. See Figure 7 for an example of a completed development plan.

Figure 7

Moe's Development Plan

NAME: Moe
MANAGER: Phyllis

Development Goal	Actions	Measures of Success	Time Frame
Rebuild relationships with all constituents so I regain their trust and respect and we accomplish the regional turnaround.	1. Immediately apologize to all for aggressive, bullying, disrespectful behavior. • Peers: request one-on-one in-person meetings with Mike, Allison, George, and Mary. Perform a stakeholder analysis so I can flex my style to theirs • Peers' teams: attend peers' staff meetings to apologize to their teams and get to know them better • Direct reports: apologize for the problems my behaviors have caused them 2. Immediately stop behaving in the manner described in action #1 above. 3. Show respect for people, their expertise, and their ideas. • In meetings, listen and don't cut people off • Remain silent twice as much as I speak • Acknowledge they are the subject matter experts • When I have a question, soften my tone of voice and approach so it comes across as a request for additional information and not as a criticism • Stop visibly showing disappointment and impatience (stop rolling eyes, sighing, frowning, and the like) • Say "thank you" for their efforts 4. Take a collaborative team approach • See action #2 below for additional actions to take to promote teamwork • Ask what I can do to support the other functions' needs to ensure them our relationship isn't just one-way • Reach out to peers and their key direct reports on the team once a week to ensure we communicate • Identify a "quick win" that we all participate in achieving and then celebrate it 5. Identify a peer who can be an "advocate" and advisor	**Short-Term** Pro-actively seek ongoing feedback from • Phyllis and Rob • Peers from other functions • Direct reports **Long-Term** • Employee engagement survey results improve (direct reports) • 360 survey results improve • My reputation is rebuilt Revenues increase and region turnaround is successful.	• Immediately, especially following key meetings and presentations • Yearly survey • Due in 6 months • One year, with progress checks periodically • By end of fiscal year
Articulate well-defined priorities to drive the turnaround and stick to them so all functions have a clear understanding of what to do.	1. Identify the three most important priorities for the turnaround 2. Discuss these with peers and direct reports to obtain their input 3. Modify as needed to show I'm listening 4. Once finalized, obtain their buy-in 5. Ensure each function understands their ultimate deliverables, timelines, and milestones 6. When I'm tempted to change courses quickly, employ the Urgent/Important tool to put ideas in perspective	• No "misunderstandings" as to what to do or order of priority • Due dates are met • Revenues increase • Priorities are "retired" and replaced with new ones on a routine basis	• Immediately • As needed

Fixes Addressed: Redefine Leadership; Measure Relevant Outcomes; Refocus on Steady Targets; Leverage Individual Differences; Treat Context as Paramount; Make Change Easier; Fix the Broken Link

Development Plan Alignment Meeting

It is crucial that the leader, coach, leader's manager, and HR sponsor be in complete agreement regarding the two to three development goals selected by the leader. This four-way meeting is a chance for the leader to present their development plan, share the reasons for the selected areas as far as the team and business impact, ask for resources and support, obtain input and suggestions, and gain overall alignment on the path forward.

Further, the alignment meeting creates ownership of the plan and the behavior modifications needed on the part of the leader because the leader is the one presenting the plan, not the coach. The coach attends to add "color commentary" and to ensure the leader is not minimizing an important finding or being too self-critical. The meeting also creates commitment on the part of the leader's manager and HR sponsor, as they feel included in the creation of the plan. The bottom line is that with this kind of clarity, there are no surprises at the end of the coaching initiative as far as what the leader is working on in relation to the expectations of the manager and HR sponsor.

Fixes Addressed: Redefine Leadership; Measure Relevant Outcomes; Refocus on Steady Targets; Leverage Individual Differences; Treat Context as Paramount; Make Change Easier; Fix the Broken Link

Phase 4: Behavior Modification and Skill-Building

Ongoing Coaching Sessions

Once the development plan is in place, coaching sessions of an hour occur once per month for approximately 5 months. The leader and coach determine their own rhythm, so sessions may be held twice a month for 30 minutes or an hour, depending on the behaviors being addressed or the leader's preferences or needs. The key is to have sessions often enough that behavior changes stay top of mind, but not so often that the leader does not have time to practice new behaviors between sessions.

It is during these sessions that the coach applies their well-honed coaching skills and utilizes their toolkit of development materials with the leader to ensure progress is being made. The coaching sessions are tailored to the leader based upon the content of the development plan and the leader's learning style. Sessions can range from the leader just using the coach as a sounding board to structured content such as role-playing an upcoming encounter or event. They usually include a discussion of progress versus the development plan and a debrief of the behavior changes the leader has tried since the last coaching session. The success or lack of success of a behavior change is discussed, and mid-course corrections are made as needed.

All sessions are designed to increase the leader's strategic self-awareness and ability to modify behaviors in service of making the team more effective.

Fixes Addressed: Redefine Leadership; Measure Relevant Outcomes; Refocus on Steady Targets; Leverage Individual Differences; Treat Context as Paramount; Make Change Easier; Fix the Broken Link

Phase 5: Evaluation and Ensuring Continued Success

Follow-up 360 Interviews

In keeping with the "Measure Relevant Outcomes" solution for which Hogan recommends quantitative measures, we recommend that at the completion of the coaching sessions that a brief follow-up 360 interview be conducted with the original respondents to evaluate the leader's progress. In these brief interviews, the coach gains the 360 respondents' perspectives on whether they have seen positive behavior changes and if they see anything left to be done. These interviews are typically 30 minutes or less, and rather than using the same questions from the original interviews, they focus on key points such as if the leader changed their behavior and the visible impact of the behavior changes on the leader's team, the leader's results, and the leader's reputation.

Fixes Addressed: Redefine Leadership; Measure Relevant Outcomes; Refocus on Steady Targets; Leverage Individual Differences; Treat Context as Paramount; Make Change Easier; Fix the Broken Link

Wrap-up Meeting

After the coach and leader have discussed the results from the follow-up 360 interviews, they meet with the leader's manager and HR sponsor for a wrap-up session. In this meeting, the leader reviews their progress versus their development plan, including what they have learned during the coaching initiative, what is going well, and what is still left to do. While the leader's perspective is important, the perspectives of the leader's manager and the HR sponsor are crucial, as they have objectively observed behavior changes and have likely gathered input from the leader's stakeholders. Further, the quantitative measures selected for the development plan are an objective indication of progress, and qualitative measures such as feedback, while not quantitative, are the perspectives of others, not self-assessments. In addition, any measure that obtains the team's perspective, such as team engagement or satisfaction, is a compelling measure.

Often, the coaching initiative is concluded because the leader has made so much progress. Sometimes the coaching initiative is extended because the leader has found it very valuable and wants to retire the original development goals and embark on new ones.

Fixes Addressed: Redefine Leadership; Measure Relevant Outcomes; Refocus on Steady Targets; Leverage Individual Differences; Treat Context as Paramount; Make Change Easier; Fix the Broken Link

Coaching Case Study: Moe

Background

Moe is a results-oriented, driven VP of Sales for a mid-sized consumer products company with a 15-year track record of success. Four months ago, he assumed responsibility for a geographic region that historically accounted for about 30% of the company's revenues. Over the last year, the company's competition has blitzed the region with discounts, innovative products, and a larger sales force, which has resulted in a significant loss of revenues (25% thus far) for Moe's territory.

The primary reason Moe was brought into the job was to turn the situation around, as he is known as "the consummate salesman" and a "real go-getter" who typically stays calm under pressure and builds solid relationships with both his clients and his colleagues. In addition, the move to a regional territory was a good developmental move for Moe, as he was an individual contributor early in his career and then ran a small team of salespeople for the last 3 years.

There is a real sense of urgency on the part of the company to replace the revenue they're losing, and Moe is looking for ways to accomplish that goal. He has set tough objectives to generate new business, and he is quite impatient when things don't move fast enough for him. He thinks that if he wants something, the entire organization (including marketing, operations, finance, IT, etc.) should drop what they're doing to accommodate his request. He has become increasingly demanding and dictatorial in his unreasonable requests and timelines, all positioned in the name of the turnaround.

Further, he changes directions frequently, and the other functions don't know what they should work on first. He is hypercritical of the other functions to the point that the operations people feel completely devalued and disrespected. They refer to encounters with him as being "Moe-ed down," and they are threatening not to meet with him anymore.

Contrasting this feedback is extremely positive feedback from his direct reports that Moe has very strong values and treats them like a family. However, they are becoming increasingly concerned that his treatment of the other functions is impacting their ability to do their jobs and achieve their goals. In addition, his constantly shifting priorities and changes in direction are confusing them.

Coach Selection

Chemistry Call

Moe conducted a chemistry call with two coaches and decided that Cynthia was the best match for him. Moe selected Cynthia because he thought he could learn the most from someone *not* like him. Cynthia came across as soft-spoken and patient, traits not attributed to Moe. However, she has an excellent business background, has a track record of success in coaching executives, and is not a "pushover," so Moe thought she would hold him accountable. He liked that about her.

Phase 1: Context Gathering

Context Call

In the context call with Phyllis (Moe's manager, who is the Senior VP of Sales) and Rob (the HR sponsor), Cynthia learned that Moe is under tremendous pressure to turn the declining revenues around. Moe's region typically accounted for about 30% of company revenues, and the regional revenue has declined 25% since the competitor started their blitz about a year ago. Phyllis explained that while she does not condone Moe's bad behavior and she is concerned that he has alienated the other functions, she understands why it could be occurring. She said when Moe was moved into the VP Sales job 4 months ago, both she and the CEO (Tom) told him to do "whatever it takes" to turn the situation around, and he's obviously doing just that. He was also told that the company was counting on him, and if he succeeded, he would move into Phyllis's SVP job when she moves to another division in a year.

Rob contributed that he thought Moe's aggressive behavior might be driven by the scope change of his assignment as well. Moe's prior sales roles over the last 15 years had been primarily individual contributor roles where he always excelled as the top salesperson. He supervised a small team of three people in his job before this one that was servicing a long-standing national account. Leading a regional organization of six direct reports and 100 people total is far more complex and definitely new to him.

Phyllis and Rob shared that coming into the job, Moe had a stellar reputation for being a top performer, energetic and enthusiastic about sales and the company, who set high goals and always delivered. People skills had never been his strong suit, but that did not matter as much in the past as it does now. His poor people skills are now a "deal breaker," as the complaints from other functions and his team have reached crisis level. Moe must change his behavior and try to reclaim his good reputation, or Phyllis will need to remove him from the job. Thus, the reason for employing a coach.

Phyllis and Rob were unsure as to whether Moe is truly coachable. When approached about coaching, Moe said he was always open to improvement, but they do not know how sincere he was. He definitely understands that his counterproductive behavior cannot continue or he will be removed from the job, so they thought that was a significant incentive for him to participate actively in the coaching.

Phyllis and Rob view Moe's interactions with the other functions as the key behaviors to modify, as the other functions are refusing to meet with him. Further, due to Moe's bullying of the other departments, his own team is suffering because the other functions do not want to meet with them either. Moe's direct reports are beginning to grumble that they can no longer do their jobs efficiently and their sales goals are in jeopardy. Their trust in Moe is deteriorating, and there are rumors that some people have put out feelers about moving to other sales teams.

Further, both Moe's direct reports and the other functions complain that his priorities seem to shift on a daily basis, and he does a poor job of communicating the changes and the reasons for them. They feel they are constantly in crisis management mode.

According to Phyllis and Rob, success would be that Moe mend fences with the other functions and develop collaborative relationships so they will support the revenue turnaround. With his own team, success would be that he regain their respect and trust and that they start to enjoy working for him. The ultimate outcome for the organization would be that they achieve their sales goals and reverse the dire revenue decline.

Get-Acquainted Call

When Cynthia met with Moe to become better acquainted, he described the same dire business situation as Phyllis and Rob. However, he really did not understand what all the fuss was about because he was just doing what the CEO and Phyllis had charged him with: "do whatever it takes" to turn the regional revenues around. He said he was promised carte blanche to do what was needed, and now that he was doing it, Phyllis and Rob were "all over him about the need to play nice" with the other functions.

Moe said if the other functions would just do their jobs, he would not need to exhibit the aggressive behaviors he was accused of. He said he was completely frustrated because he seemed to be the only person with a sense of urgency about turning the region around. He added that the other functions weren't very agile, as they were having a hard time shifting gears when priorities changed due to pressing business needs.

He shared that in the past, he had been told that his key strengths were his ability to deliver results (setting stretch goals and pursuing them fearlessly) and his ability to build solid customer relationships. He also said that in the past, he hadn't had any problems building relationships with his colleagues and direct reports. He said he thought his areas for development were impatience and coming on too strong sometimes.

Moe's view of success was to restore relationships with the other functions so they would do what he needed them to do to achieve the turnaround. When Cynthia questioned him about his team, he was not aware of any issues. He said, "they know I love them—we're like one big, happy family."

Phase 2: Assessment and Feedback

Hogan Assessments and 360 Interviews

During the get-acquainted meeting, Cynthia explained the importance of having a baseline of assessment as the foundation for the coaching initiative. She explained that Moe would complete the three Hogan assessments (HPI, HDS, and MVPI), and to complement those, she would be conducting 360 interviews with a select group of respondents he, Phyllis, and Rob agreed upon. Cynthia and Moe reviewed typical 360 interview questions and decided on an appropriate set for Cynthia to ask. Moe identified Phyllis, the CEO, four peers, and four direct reports to be his audience, and Phyllis and Rob subsequently approved the list. In addition, they approved the 360 interview questions for Cynthia to pose. See Appendix 4 for the list of 360 interview questions agreed upon.

Moe took the Hogan assessments immediately upon receiving the log-in information, and Cynthia completed the 360 interviews over the following 2 weeks. They then met for the integrated feedback session.

Integrated Feedback Session

Hogan LFS Feedback

Cynthia began the integrated feedback session by covering Moe's Hogan assessment results, using the Flash Report as the centerpiece. See

Appendix 5 for Moe's Flash Report. The key themes Cynthia discussed with Moe were the following:

- Confident, driven, and leader-like with a focus on making a contribution and achieving results. Under pressure, might come on too strong, overcommit, be demanding, or blame others. (high Adjustment, Ambition, Power, and Bold)

- Direct, frank, and purposeful communicator who might tend to be more business-focused and task-focused than people-focused. Under stress, might be seen as withdrawn, cold, aloof, or as "losing his humanity." (low Sociability and Interpersonal Sensitivity, higher Reserved, and low Altruism and Affiliation)

- Practical and principled leader who will likely value order and maintain high standards. Might need to ensure he doesn't discourage innovation and new ideas. Interested in doing what is "right" for the organization and customers. (low Inquisitive, moderate Prudence, lower Imaginative, high Security and Tradition)

- Under stress, might become distracted and resort to crisis management (higher Excitable, Colorful, and lower subscales under Prudence)

Cynthia pointed out that the results were generally consistent with what she heard from the 360 interview respondents, which they would discuss subsequently.

Moe thought the Hogan results were accurate for the most part. He agreed with his key strengths and possible derailing behaviors, but he minimized the impact of his derailers, saying he thought they were appropriate given the extreme challenge he faced.

360 Interviews Feedback

The input from the respondents reinforced Moe's Hogan assessment results. Further, the feedback revealed how destructive Moe's behavior was to others and how serious the implications were for the business and Moe's reputation. Appendix 3 is Cynthia's detailed summary of the 360 interviews, containing all respondents' feedback in a bulleted format. To protect confidentiality, the individual groups are not identified as direct reports, peers, or managers.

However, Cynthia saw clear but slightly different themes from the three groups, and she used these in her analysis and feedback to Moe, even though she didn't attribute them to particular respondents:

Managers (Phyllis, SVP Sales and Moe's manager, and Tom, CEO and Phyllis's manager)

Phyllis and Tom both said they bore some responsibility for Moe's aggressive behavior, as they told him to do "whatever it takes" to turn the revenue situation around. They viewed his aggressive behavior as his version of what was necessary to accomplish the goal. They said they expected him to "ruffle a few feathers," but now that his peers and their teams were refusing to work with him, they were gravely concerned that the revenue situation would worsen. Further, they commented that Moe must be under more pressure than they anticipated because his extreme behaviors were very unlike the Moe they had observed in the past. Phyllis said she felt her leadership was being questioned by her peers because she wasn't controlling Moe. Tom agreed and said Phyllis's peers were grumbling to him about Moe and Phyllis's apparent inability to rein him in, and the entire C-suite team was being negatively impacted.

Cynthia's takeaway was that they admired Moe's sense of urgency, enthusiasm, and commitment around reversing the revenue slippage and they thought his more direct communication style was needed, but he had just gone too far.

Peers (function heads: Mike, IT; Allison, marketing; George, manufacturing; Mary, installation)

Moe's peers were very consistent in their feedback, and among the three respondent groups, they were the most unforgiving of his behavior. They said he was boorish, intimidating, and disrespectful to them and their teams. When he didn't like their suggestions or when they missed a due date because of extenuating circumstances, he humiliated and belittled them. Further, they said Moe was a credit hog—when things went well, he portrayed it as being all because of him, and when something went wrong, he was quick to blame others. They and their teams had started calling his presentations the "Moe show," and they referred to interactions with him as being "Moe-ed over" or "Moe-ed down." They said they were looking to him to be the leader of the interfunctional turnaround team, but he had sorely disappointed them with his boorish behavior.

They said his priorities changed on a daily basis ("crisis management at its finest" per one peer), and their teams were completely confused as to where their focus should be. They would leave one of Moe's meetings thinking they should do one thing, and when they delivered it, he would explode and rant about how it wasn't what they should have been working on. They said at first they overlooked the bullying because they knew he was under a lot of pressure and he just wasn't himself. While they hadn't worked closely with him in the past, he had always been cordial and they had enjoyed their interactions, but now they were dealing with a completely different Moe.

Cynthia's takeaway was that relationships were so badly damaged that it would take a monumental effort on Moe's part to repair them. She felt the peers were very skeptical that he could do it or would even want to do it. They advised her that he was uncoachable and wished her luck.

Direct Reports (regional sales reps: Jorge, Ashley, Maria, Daniel)

Moe's direct reports' feedback was consistent in that they all described two different Moes. They said in many ways, he treated them like family—concerned about their personal welfare and supportive of them in their careers. They also saw the aggressive, bullying side of Moe in his interactions with the other functions, and they were embarrassed by it. His behavior was impacting the direct reports, not because he exhibited the extreme behaviors to them, but because the other functions were shutting them out, and they couldn't do their jobs effectively. They described it as "guilt by association"—Moe was so disliked that it was rubbing off on them. Several said they or other sales reps felt it was time to move to another sales team.

Further, they said that recently, Moe had begun changing priorities so frequently that they really didn't understand what they should focus on. They felt they were always putting out fires.

Cynthia's takeaway was that Moe needed to think of his team through the leadership lens of building and maintaining a high-performing team, and not just through the lens of how he treated them.

Combining the feedback detailed in Appendix 3 and the information above, Cynthia identified the following the key themes to discuss with Moe:

- While respondents said Moe had some towering strengths of being results-oriented, driven, customer-focused, concerned about doing the right thing, and a consummate sales professional, his aggressive behavior was so offensive that it was totally outweighing these strengths, causing people to become very disillusioned about him.

- His reputation, which had been stellar until he assumed the regional Sales VP role, was rapidly deteriorating to the point that people didn't want to work with him. Ironically, the behaviors he was employing to spur the turnaround were having the opposite effect and severely negatively impacting it because people were actively and passive-aggressively ignoring him.

- His team of direct reports was being negatively impacted because of his behaviors. Other departments were ignoring the team's requests in order to thwart Moe's success. Moe needed to recognize that he was letting his team down and that leadership involved more than just being the manager of the group.

Given the consistency and intensity of the feedback, Moe couldn't deny it. At first, he was defensive and said he didn't think his behavior was out of line. He thought people were exaggerating the extent of his aggressiveness and "making a mountain out of a molehill." Cynthia spoke with him about the importance of strategic self-awareness and how others see him, and the implications for his reputation and future career. He reluctantly acknowledged that it was other people's perceptions that mattered and not how he intended his actions. Moe was anxious to get promoted, and he said he was willing to "play the game" of modifying his behavior if it would get him off the hot seat.

Moe agreed to process the feedback and reflect on what he thought he should do to address it, and he and Cynthia agreed to meet the next week to start outlining actions in a development plan. Between now and then, though, he agreed to try to soften his behavior to see if he could achieve an early win.

Phase 3: Development Planning

Development Planning Meeting

Moe reflected on the integrated feedback over the next week, and he and Cynthia then met to continue their discussion. They agreed that in terms of the Hogan Leadership Model, modifications to Moe's behaviors associated with the Interpersonal domain (Connection and Influence dimensions) and the Intrapersonal domain (Humility dimension) were the ones that would most positively impact his effectiveness. Together, they identified two critical development areas that would form the crux of Moe's development plan:

1. The need to quickly rebuild relationships, both with his peers in other functions and their teams and with his own team.

2. The need to be more clear on priorities, expectations, and due dates, and once established, stop changing them so frequently.

Both these areas would involve radically modifying his behavior immediately, and Moe recognized this would take significant effort and commitment on his part.

Moe agreed to draft a development plan to expound on these areas that would include the elements of a good development plan that Cynthia explained to him (e.g., definition of success, specific actions to take, support needed, measures, and timelines). Further, Cynthia continued to reinforce the definition of leadership as it relates to teams so he would focus his development plan on the success of his teams (both his direct report team and his cross-functional turnaround team) and not solely on his success. They agreed to meet again in a week to finalize the plan.

Development Plan Finalization Meeting

Moe drafted a development plan addressing the two areas he and Cynthia had identified, and he emailed it to her for suggestions and comments. They then met to finalize it (see Figure 7 on page 37 for Moe's development plan). They also discussed an agenda for the upcoming alignment meeting with Phyllis and Rob to gain their input and concurrence, including, that it was Moe's meeting to share his learnings and development plan, and that Cynthia would provide "color commentary" as needed.

Development Planning Alignment Meeting

Moe and Cynthia met the following week with Phyllis and Rob to obtain their input and to ensure their full alignment with and support of the development plan. Moe was especially interested in ensuring their advocacy for him, as he was in "recovery mode" with his stakeholders. Phyllis and Rob approved the development plan with no changes and agreed categorically to advocate for him with his constituents and to provide him with ongoing feedback as he changed his behaviors.

Phase 4: Behavior Modification and Skill-Building

Ongoing Coaching Sessions

Cynthia and Moe agreed to meet twice a month (eight sessions) over the next 4 months given the urgency of the situation and the need for Moe to practice new behaviors and debrief about them more often than once per month.

Once Moe had the wake-up call from the integrated feedback session and realized how toxic he had become, in true Moe form, he committed to changing his behavior immediately. He knew it would be difficult because of his strong desire to accomplish the revenue turnaround, but Cynthia helped him re-frame his behavior and the need to get the other functions on board as a key component of the turnaround. Over the next 4 months, Moe and Cynthia engaged in the following:

1. To start, he and Cynthia role-played how he would approach each of his key stakeholders to thank them for their input to the 360 (if they had been one of the respondents), to offer an individual apology, and to commit to interacting with them differently in the future. Cynthia and Moe discussed that sincerity was key and approaching each stakeholder on their own terms was critical. Therefore, they performed a stakeholder analysis to ensure he flexed his style to theirs.

2. The negative impact Moe was having on his team was a true blind spot for him. Cynthia helped him change his leadership lens from one of being in charge of the team to one of empowering and motivating them to outperform the competition. He realized that if he rebuilt relationships with the other functions and clarified priorities, his own direct reports would be beneficiaries.

3. Cynthia helped Moe reframe his interactions with the other functions. Essentially, he was the leader of the turnaround initiative, and even though the other functions didn't report to him, he was the de facto leader and needed to behave in a way to facilitate their success.

4. Moe and Cynthia identified Moe's "triggers" and how to anticipate them and therefore mitigate his negative behaviors. Moe felt his impatience to turn the region's revenue around was his key trigger. He also admitted that when he didn't agree with a solution proposed by the other functions, it set him off. He committed to listening more and being more open-minded about new ideas. He and Cynthia practiced his reactions and ways to phrase questions and comments so he didn't sound so adversarial in his delivery. They also worked on his non-verbals—body language and facial expressions.

5. Moe immediately identified three key priorities for the turnaround and set about gaining input and concurrence from the stakeholders. Once done, he created a tracking mechanism for each task so stakeholders could update progress and all knew where they stood.

6. Cynthia and Moe spoke at length about the culture he wanted to foster as the leader and the reputation he wanted to create for himself and his team. He shared his vision with his direct reports and other stakeholders and asked for ongoing feedback. He and Cynthia agreed he would use this as an "acid test" to ensure his behavior was consistent with achieving it.

7. Cynthia helped Moe identify an early win that would reinforce how his more productive behaviors had had a positive impact, help him gain credibility with his stakeholders that he was serious about changing, and re-energize the organization. Moe selected an upcoming large sale to a major client that was highly competitive that would be a real coup to win.

8. Input from all 360 respondents was that Moe had excellent customer relationship skills. He was known to always listen, to be polite and "unflappable," and to be collaborative in solving problems with customers. Cynthia worked with him to use how he treated customers as a benchmark for how he should treat his peers and their teams. Further, his direct reports described how caring

and concerned he could be about them, so Cynthia helped him translate those skills to his peers and other colleagues as well.

9. Moe acknowledged he was more stressed than he had ever been. Because of the long hours he was working, he had discontinued his workouts at the gym, and they had always been a stress release for him. He started working out again to combat stress.

10. Moe identified two trusted colleagues he could use as a sounding board for decisions and also from whom he could get straight feedback regarding his behaviors.

In each coaching session, Cynthia and Moe discussed his progress versus his development plan and debriefed the meetings and interactions he had had with stakeholders since their last session.

At first, the new behaviors were completely foreign to Moe, and there were several times he reverted to aggressive behaviors. However, as he received feedback from his stakeholders on how much better they liked the "new Moe," his new behaviors were reinforced. Further, revenue results improved, and there was substantially less "drama" in the organization. After accomplishing the early win Moe had identified, he hosted a celebration and openly thanked all functions for their role in achieving this result.

Phase 5: Evaluation and Ensuring Continued Success

Follow-up 360 Interviews

At the end of the 6-month initiative, Cynthia conducted brief follow-up calls with the same 360 respondents to determine Moe's progress. When interviewed, all respondents said they had seen a significant change for the better. Several said their hats were off to Moe because they knew how much effort it takes to change. Several said they hoped Moe's good behaviors would continue, but they needed to see them for a longer period of time to be completely convinced that he was a changed man. Revenues were beginning to recover, and they attributed this to people now wanting to support Moe rather than thwart him.

Wrap-up Meeting

To bring closure to the initiative, Moe, Cynthia, Phyllis, and Rob met to discuss what had been accomplished and what was left to do. Moe reviewed his progress versus his development plan and shared he thought he had made great progress based on anecdotal feedback, the 360 follow-up interviews, and the promising revenue figures that had begun to materialize. Phyllis and Rob agreed and advised that if Moe stayed on the same trajectory, he would once again be a candidate for Phyllis's job when she left for a different division in a year. They cautioned him that while he had made remarkable progress, people have long memories and he needed to ensure he didn't backslide, thereby eliciting sentiments of "we knew the changes wouldn't last."

Cynthia suggested that Phyllis and Rob conduct a written 360 survey on Moe in 6 months. Further, the organization's annual employee engagement survey was to be conducted in 4 months, so Cynthia encouraged them to use this as a measure of his progress.

Moe expressed his appreciation to Cynthia for her help and guidance. He felt that he had grown tremendously from his work with her and that he was self-sufficient enough at this point to sustain his behavior changes without extending the coaching initiative.

Epilogue

Moe continued to be hyperaware of how he was coming across to others so he wouldn't fall into his bad behaviors again. He maintained his workout routine to relieve stress, and he sought ongoing feedback from a few trusted colleagues. It took about a year for the region to regain the 25% revenues they had lost, and when they crossed that threshold, Moe celebrated the success and gave credit to the broad team that was involved. Several of Moe's former detractors sent him emails of congratulations for leading the charge. Shortly after, Phyllis was promoted to a different division, and Moe became her replacement.

Endnotes

[1]Robert Hogan, Robert Raskin, and Dan Fazzini, "The Dark Side of Charisma" in *Measures of Leadership,* ed. K. E. Clark and M. B. Clark (West Orange, NJ: Leadership Library of America, Inc., 1990), 343–354.

[2]Frederick Herzberg, "One More Time: How Do You Motivate Employees?," *Harvard Business Review*, no. 46 (1968): 53–62, https://hbr.org/2003/01/one-more-time-how-do-you-motivate-employees; Frederick Hertzberg, Bernard Mausner, and Barbara B. Snyderman, *The Motivation to Work* New York: John Wiley and Sons, (1959).

[3]https://www.gallop.com/workplace/349484/state-of-the-global-workplace.aspx

[4]Meghan Casserly, (2012, October 17). "Majority of Americans Would Rather Fire their Boss than Get a Raise," *Forbes,* https://www.forbes.com/sites/meghancasserly/2012/10/17/majority-of-americans-would-rather-fire-their-boss-than-get-a-raise/?sh=69f370f96610.

[5]https://pubmed.nobi.nih.gov/10096996

[6]2021 DDI Global Leadership Forecast.

Appendices

Appendix 1: Coach's Notes from a Context Meeting

February 3, 202X

Initiative: 6-month coaching for Stan (Store Manager of a big-box store)

In attendance: Coach: Dan; **Stan's Manager:** Mirna (Region Manager); **Stan's HR Sponsor:** Jeff

Primary reason for coaching: *Mirna said Stan has been with the company for 12 years and has been a solid performer the entire time. He started in a smaller store and was moved to successively larger stores because his results were so good. He has been working for Mirna for 3 years, and in that time, he's been a top performer with stellar operating results, and his team loves him. She thinks he has potential to be her successor, but some higher-level managers don't think he has enough executive presence. He's quiet and doesn't actively speak up in meetings. When Mirna encourages him to be more vocal, he says his results should speak for themselves. Jeff agreed with Mirna and added that he thinks Stan is "naïve" as far as corporate politics go, and he needs to realize he has to "play the game" and be more assertive if he wants to get ahead.*

Key strengths, development areas, and blind spots: *Both cited Stan's balance of task and people as a towering strength ("just a nice guy"). Development area as mentioned above to have more executive presence, be more assertive, speak up more, have more visibility with executives. Jeff reiterated that Stan's naivete is a blind spot.*

Reputation: *Stan is known as a solid performer and an expert in store-related matters. His peers look to him for guidance and leadership; they trust him. He's a "quiet leader" who shares credit with his team. He's known to be reliable and loyal to the company. He's well-liked by employees and customers alike.*

Behavior change with most positive impact on team: *The behavior changes described above are the ones that would have the most positive impact on the team because if Stan becomes more vocal and visible, their work would be more visible. Executives would know what a great job the team is doing. This could provide additional career opportunities for them.*

Culture: *Mirna and Jeff described the company as a paradox—on the one hand, it's folksy and down-home and very unpretentious, but on the other hand, the executives expect the rising stars to be polished, articulate, and sophisticated.*

Stan's attitude toward coaching: *Stan looks forward to having a coach and to improving in any way he can. That said, he thinks it's a shame his work and his team's work don't speak for themselves and therefore he has to put "window dressing" on it.*

How to define success of the coaching initiative: *Stan will exhibit more executive presence, be more vocal, be more comfortable around the higher-ups, toot his own horn and his team's horn more (without being obnoxious about it); higher-ups would agree he's a viable successor for Mirna.*

Appendix 2: Typical 360 Interview Questions

1. Describe _____'s greatest strengths. How do these enhance _____'s effectiveness or ability to achieve business objectives?

2. What are _____'s areas that need further development? Describe an event in which you observed the development need in action. How did this hinder _____'s effectiveness or ability to achieve business objectives?

3. How would you describe _____'s reputation?

4. How self-aware is _____?

5. How would you describe _____'s leadership style?

6. How would you describe _____'s communication style?

7. How does _____ develop people?

8. How effective is _____ interpersonally:
   a. with direct reports?
   b. with peers?
   c. with immediate manager?
   d. with other senior managers?

9. How would you characterize _____'s decision-making style?

10. What kind of team player is _____?

11. How does _____ use their power and influence?

12. How does _____ deal with stressful situations?

13. How effective is _____ in developing a strategic view for their business area?

14. What would you say about _____'s future in the company (e.g., how do you see them making the best contribution to the organization)?

15. What major obstacles do you see facing _____ in their career?

16. What are the things that make people successful in this organization?

17. Apart from _____'s areas needing further work, what organizational issues exist here?

18. How do these organizational issues affect _____'s performance, or do they?

19. What are the key relationships that _____ needs to manage? How would you characterize these relationships today?

20. If you could tell _____ to **start** doing one thing, what would it be? To **keep** doing one thing, what would it be? To **stop** doing one thing, what would it be?

21. Do you have any other comments or observations that would contribute to _____'s developmental work?

Note: Time usually doesn't permit the coach to ask all the above questions, and in some cases, certain questions aren't applicable to the leader's context or to the respondents, so the coach needs to consult with the leader, the leader's manager, and the HR sponsor to determine which questions are the most appropriate.

Examples include eliminating question 13 if the leader isn't involved in strategy setting or asking question 7 only of direct reports if peers or the manager don't have sufficient visibility into how the leader develops their people.

Further, questions can be customized if the leader, the manager, or the HR sponsor have a particular behavior or capability for which they'd like insights to facilitate the leader's effectiveness. An example is a leader who was afraid he overused his sense of humor and wasn't taken seriously, so the coach asked, "Does John overuse his sense of humor? If so, how, and how does it impact his effectiveness?"

Appendix 3: Summary of Moe's 360 Interviews

Strengths

Personal/leadership presence: confident, dynamic, energetic, passionate, upbeat, enthusiastic

Results-orientation: want to win, competitive, hard-working, deliver on commitments, execute well

Business knowledge: understand the business, the market, the competitors

Values: family-oriented, and apply this to work family; want to do right thing; very loyal to the company

Rose to the occasion in a very tough situation

Great job with customers: they love you; consummate sales person

Areas for Development

Competitive to the extreme: laser focus on achieving YOUR goals, and dead bodies are left in the wake; come across as self-promoting ("the Moe show"); always "selling"

Aggressive behavior when people don't meet your expectations; harsh in criticism of people; they feel disrespected and de-valued ("Moe-ed over")

Pushing people too hard: "bullying"; people don't want to go the extra mile for you—in fact it's to the point that they're sabotaging you; unreasonable requests and deadlines; your way or the highway, all in the name of the turnaround

Constantly shifting priorities: people don't know from day to day what they should focus on because you change your mind so often

Unclear communications: when priorities change, you don't communicate why; people are lost

Too many fire drills: you're constantly redirecting people from one crisis to the next

Relationship building:

1. *Lower levels in other functions: feel devalued and disrespected*
2. *Peers in other functions: feel bullied; tired of you using the turnaround as a hammer*

Reputation

Very favorable until you took this job, and now it is deteriorating rapidly

Not favorable with other departments ("bully"), and your direct reports are suffering from this

Level of Self-Awareness

Fairly self-aware, but might not care in the heat of the moment

Leadership Style

High expectations

Results-driven

Confident

With direct reports, seem to be caring and collaborative

With others, "do what I say," dictatorial, adversarial

Communication Style

Can deliver tough messages

Excellent speaker when calm

Very intimidating and demeaning when upset

Don't explain rationale for frequent changes of priorities very well

Interpersonal Effectiveness

Good with upper management, direct reports, and customers

Terrible with peers and their teams

Decision-Making Style

Quick, and even impulsive at times

Sometimes fact-based and data-driven

Make decisions yourself—always have a move in mind

Need to get input

Overly confident—you don't know everything

Don't care about people's feelings

Team Player

Good with own team

Nonexistent with other functions

Act in self-interest

Take credit yourself rather than sharing it with the interfunctional team

Handling Stressful Situations

Remain cool, calm, and upbeat with customers

Become agitated and aggressive with peers and their teams

Key Relationships

Direct reports: great, but they're concerned about your behavior to the other functions

Phyllis and higher-ups: okay, but they're beginning to hear damaging things about you from their teams

Peers and their teams: poor and getting worse

Customers: excellent

Start Doing

Remaining calm when you don't get your way

Repairing and building relationships with other functions

Showing other functions you genuinely appreciate the work they're doing to support you

Leveraging the other functions' expertise; respect what they recommend

Sticking with priorities

Communicating reasons for rapidly shifting focus

Thanking people—it will go a long way

Stop Doing

Bullying and humiliating people

Acting so aggressively

Questioning everyone's judgment

Being disrespectful

Coming on so strong

Changing priorities so frequently

Keep Doing

Being positive, passionate, and results-focused

Pushing the team to deliver results (but do it differently)

Focusing on the scoreboard (but not to the exclusion of everything else)

Being customer-centric

Appendix 4: Moe's 360 Interview Questions

1. Describe Moe's greatest strengths. How do these enhance Moe's effectiveness or ability to achieve business objectives?

2. What are Moe's areas that need further development? Describe an event in which you observed the development need in action. How did this hinder Moe's effectiveness or ability to achieve business objectives?

3. How would you describe Moe's reputation?

4. How self-aware is Moe?

5. How would you describe Moe's leadership style?

6. How would you describe Moe's communication style?

7. How effective is Moe interpersonally:
   a. with direct reports?
   b. with peers?
   c. with immediate manager?
   d. with other senior managers?

8. How would you characterize Moe's decision-making style?

9. What kind of team player is Moe?

10. How does Moe deal with stressful situations?

11. What are the key relationships that Moe needs to manage? How would you characterize these relationships today?

12. If you could tell Moe to **start** doing one thing, what would it be? To **keep** doing one thing, what would it be? To **stop** doing one thing, what would it be?

13. Do you have any other comments or observations that would contribute to Moe's developmental work?

Appendix 5: Moe's Flash Report

HOGAN   Moe

Flash Report

Norms: Global

HPI Hogan Personality Inventory

Adjustment	88
Ambition	79
Sociability	32
Interpersonal Sensitivity	18
Prudence	51
Inquisitive	4
Learning Approach	45

HDS Hogan Development Survey

Excitable	85
Skeptical	21
Cautious	10
Reserved	88
Leisurely	3
Bold	81
Mischievous	49
Colorful	79
Imaginative	34
Diligent	53
Dutiful	13

MVPI Motives, Values, Preferences Inventory

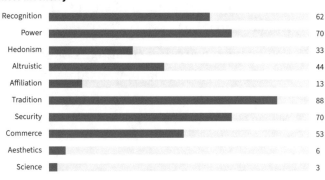

Recognition	62
Power	70
Hedonism	33
Altruistic	44
Affiliation	13
Tradition	88
Security	70
Commerce	53
Aesthetics	6
Science	3

Moe

HPI

Subscale Scores

Validity

Adjustment
Empathy
Not Anxious
No Guilt
Calmness
Even-tempered
No Complaints
Trusting
Good Attachment

Ambition
Competitive
Self-confident
Accomplishment
Leadership
Identity
No Social Anxiety

Sociability
Likes Parties
Likes Crowds
Experience Seeking
Exhibitionistic
Entertaining

Interpersonal Sensitivity
Easy To Live With
Sensitive
Caring
Likes People
No Hostility

Prudence
Moralistic
Mastery
Virtuous
Not Autonomous
Not Spontaneous
Impulse Control
Avoids Trouble

Inquisitive
Science Ability
Curiosity
Thrill Seeking
Intellectual Games
Generates Ideas
Culture

Learning Approach
Education
Math Ability
Good Memory
Reading

HDS

Subscale Scores

Excitable
Volatile
Easily Disappointed
No Direction

Skeptical
Cynical
Mistrusting
Grudges

Cautious
Avoidant
Fearful
Unassertive

Reserved
Introverted
Unsocial
Tough

Leisurely
Passive Aggressive
Unappreciated
Irritated

Bold
Entitled
Overconfidence
Fantasized Talent

Mischievous
Risky
Impulsive
Manipulative

Colorful
Public Confidence
Distractible
Self-display

Imaginative
Eccentric
Special Sensitivity
Creative Thinking

Diligent
Standards
Perfectionistic
Organized

Dutiful
Indecisive
Ingratiating
Conforming

MVPI

Subscale Scores

Recognition
Lifestyle
Beliefs
Occupational Preferences
Aversions
Preferred Associates

Power
Lifestyle
Beliefs
Occupational Preferences
Aversions
Preferred Associates

Hedonism
Lifestyle
Beliefs
Occupational Preferences
Aversions
Preferred Associates

Altruistic
Lifestyle
Beliefs
Occupational Preferences
Aversions
Preferred Associates

Affiliation
Lifestyle
Beliefs
Occupational Preferences
Aversions
Preferred Associates

Tradition
Lifestyle
Beliefs
Occupational Preferences
Aversions
Preferred Associates

Security
Lifestyle
Beliefs
Occupational Preferences
Aversions
Preferred Associates

Commerce
Lifestyle
Beliefs
Occupational Preferences
Aversions
Preferred Associates

Aesthetics
Lifestyle
Beliefs
Occupational Preferences
Aversions
Preferred Associates

Science
Lifestyle
Beliefs
Occupational Preferences
Aversions
Preferred Associates

About the Authors

Trish Kellett is the director of the Hogan Coaching Network (HCN), a team of over 60 highly experienced coaches worldwide who are experts in using the Hogan suite of personality assessments as a foundation for improving the performance of leaders, their teams, and their broader organizations. Prior to joining Hogan in 2010 to lead the HCN, Trish spent 15 years in the leadership assessment, development, and coaching industry as a consultant. Prior to that, she held executive positions at AT&T and National Service Industries in line management across multiple functions. She is the coauthor of *Coaching the Dark Side of Personality* and *Reputation: A Leader's Path to Career Success*. Trish holds a bachelor's degree in mathematics from Duke University, an MBA from the University of Miami, and she completed the residential Program for Management Development at the Harvard Business School. She lives in Vero Beach, Florida with her husband.

Jackie VanBroekhoven Sahm is the vice president of Integrated Solutions at Hogan Assessment Systems, where she oversees the innovation, design, delivery, and execution of Hogan's worldwide learning and development solutions. Jackie has over 16 years of experience working in the field of talent management and leadership development. Prior to her current role, Jackie held two director-level roles leading Hogan's Global Learning function, and later, Interactive Product Development. She also spent 10 years in a variety of senior consulting roles, first supporting large global consulting partners, then on Hogan's Corporate Solutions Team working with Fortune 500 companies in the U.S. and around the world. She holds a bachelor's of psychology from the University of Florida and a graduate degree in industrial/organizational psychology from the University of Tulsa. She lives in Tampa, Florida with her husband, two beautiful children, Luke (6) and Summer (4), and their rescue pup, Lola.

Made in United States
Troutdale, OR
06/08/2025

31977191R00049